# Assessment Book

**Editorial Offices:** Glenview, Illinois • Parsippany, New Jersey • New York, New York
**Sales Offices:** Parsippany, New Jersey • Duluth, Georgia • Glenview, Illinois
Coppell, Texas • Ontario, California

www.sfsocialstudies.com

## Program Authors

**Dr. Candy Dawson Boyd**
Professor, School of Education
Director of Reading Programs
St. Mary's College
Moraga, California

**Dr. Geneva Gay**
Professor of Education
University of Washington
Seattle, Washington

**Rita Geiger**
Director of Social Studies and
    Foreign Languages
Norman Public Schools
Norman, Oklahoma

**Dr. James B. Kracht**
Associate Dean for
    Undergraduate Programs
    and Teacher Education
College of Education
Texas A & M University
College Station, Texas

**Dr. Valerie Ooka Pang**
Professor of Teacher Education
San Diego State University
San Diego, California

**Dr. C. Frederick Risinger**
Director, Professional
    Development and Social
    Studies Education
Indiana University
Bloomington, Indiana

**Sara Miranda Sanchez**
Elementary and Early
    Childhood Curriculum
    Coordinator
Albuquerque Public Schools
Albuquerque, New Mexico

---

## Contributing Authors

**Dr. Carol Berkin**
Professor of History
Baruch College and the
    Graduate Center
The City University of New York
New York, New York

**Lee A. Chase**
Staff Development Specialist
Chesterfield County
    Public Schools
Chesterfield County, Virginia

**Dr. James Cummins**
Professor of Curriculum
Ontario Institute for Studies
    in Education
University of Toronto
Toronto, Canada

**Dr. Allen D. Glenn**
Professor and Dean Emeritus
College of Education
Curriculum and Instruction
University of Washington
Seattle, Washington

**Dr. Carole L. Hahn**
Professor, Educational Studies
Emory University
Atlanta, Georgia

**Dr. M. Gail Hickey**
Professor of Education
Indiana University-Purdue
    University
Ft. Wayne, Indiana

**Dr. Bonnie Meszaros**
Associate Director
Center for Economic Education
    and Entrepreneurship
University of Delaware
Newark, Delaware

ISBN 0-328-03091-0

**Copyright © Pearson Education, Inc.**
All rights reserved. Printed in the United States of America. The blackline masters in this publication are designed for use with appropriate equipment to reproduce copies for classroom use only. Scott Foresman grants permission to classroom teachers to reproduce from these masters.

1 2 3 4 5 6 7 8 9 10-V016-11 10 09 08 07 06 05 04 03 02

# Contents

**Unit 1:** Time for School
Content Test . . . . . . . . . . . . . . . . . . . . . . . . . . . . . 1–2
Skills Test . . . . . . . . . . . . . . . . . . . . . . . . . . . . . . . 3–4

**Unit 2:** In My Community
Content Test . . . . . . . . . . . . . . . . . . . . . . . . . . . . . 5–6
Skills Test . . . . . . . . . . . . . . . . . . . . . . . . . . . . . . . 7–8

**Unit 3:** Work! Work! Work!
Content Test . . . . . . . . . . . . . . . . . . . . . . . . . . . . . 9–10
Skills Test . . . . . . . . . . . . . . . . . . . . . . . . . . . . . . . 11–12

**Unit 4:** Our Earth, Our Resources
Content Test . . . . . . . . . . . . . . . . . . . . . . . . . . . . . 13–14
Skills Test . . . . . . . . . . . . . . . . . . . . . . . . . . . . . . . 15–16

**Unit 5:** This Is Our Country
Content Test . . . . . . . . . . . . . . . . . . . . . . . . . . . . . 17–18
Skills Test . . . . . . . . . . . . . . . . . . . . . . . . . . . . . . . 19–20

**Unit 6:** Our Country, Our World
Content Test . . . . . . . . . . . . . . . . . . . . . . . . . . . . . 21–22
Skills Test . . . . . . . . . . . . . . . . . . . . . . . . . . . . . . . 23–24

**Answer Key** . . . . . . . . . . . . . . . . . . . . . . . . . . . . 25–30

# To the Teacher

One way to evaluate the success of your social studies instruction lies in using the assessment options provided in **Scott Foresman** *Social Studies*. These options will help you measure students' progress toward social studies instructional goals.

The assessment tools provided with **Scott Foresman** *Social Studies* can

- help you determine which students need more help and where classroom instruction needs to be reinforced, reviewed, or expanded.
- help you evaluate how well students comprehend, communicate, and apply what they have learned.

**Scott Foresman** *Social Studies* provides a comprehensive assessment package as shown below.

## Assessment Options Available in Scott Foresman *Social Studies*

| | |
|---|---|
| **Formal Assessments** | ✓ What did you learn? PE/TE<br>✓ Unit Review, PE/TE<br>✓ Unit Tests, Assessment Book<br>✓ Test Talk Practice Book |
| **Informal Assessments** | ✓ Teacher's Edition Questions<br>✓ Close and Assess, TE<br>✓ Try it! PE/TE<br>✓ Think and Share, PE/TE<br>✓ Courage in Action, PE/TE<br>✓ Hands-on History, PE/TE |
| **Portfolio Assessments** | ✓ Portfolio Assessment, TE<br>✓ Leveled Practice, TE<br>✓ Workbook Pages<br>✓ Unit Review, PE/TE<br>✓ Curriculum Connection, TE |
| **Performance Assessments** | ✓ Hands-on Unit Project, PE/TE<br>✓ Internet Activity, PE<br>✓ Unit Review: Think and Share, PE/TE<br>✓ Scoring Guides, TE |

# Overview of Assessment Book

## Unit Tests

The Unit Tests are a tool to evaluate students' understanding of social studies concepts and their ability to apply and analyze the concepts. There is a four-page, reproducible test for each unit in the Student Book.

Students are asked to fill in blanks, complete sentences, choose a correct answer from a series of possible responses, draw an answer, match items, and read/complete a map, chart, or graph.

Some of the questions carry the same Test Prep symbol as found in the Student Book. The icon tells students that a particular question is formatted the same way it would appear on a standardized test.

At the back of the Assessment Book, there is an answer key for each Unit Test.

### Part 1: Content Test
The two-page content test includes a series of multiple choice questions covering levels of thinking from knowledge to comprehension, application, and analysis.

### Part 2: Skills Test
The two-page skills test checks students' knowledge of and ability to apply the social studies skills taught in the Student Book.

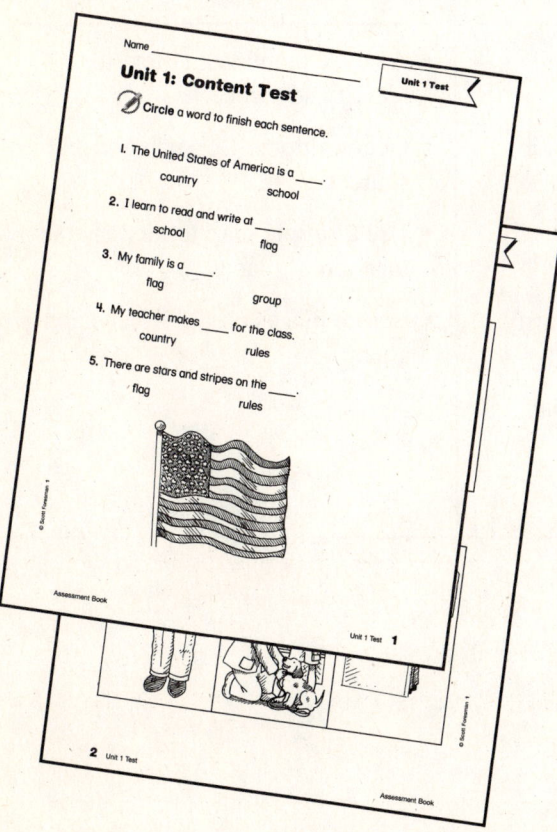
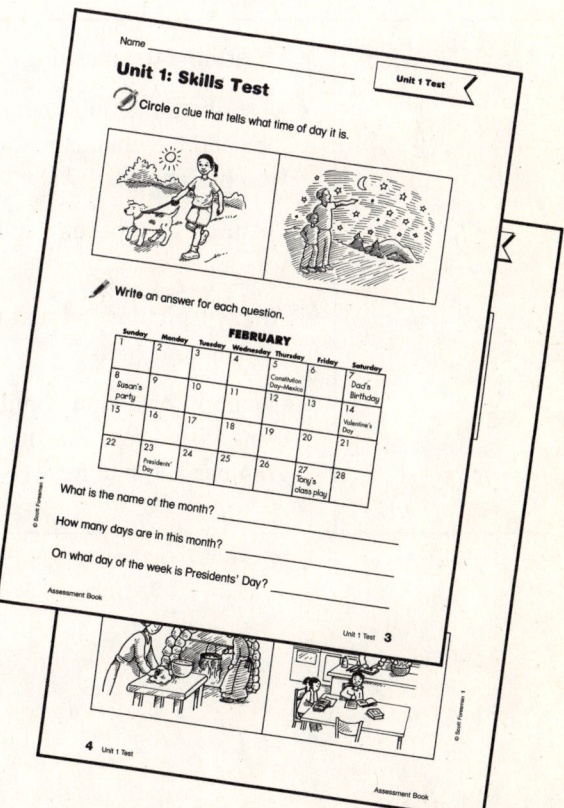

# Unit Tests: Objectives Assessed

|  | **Content Objectives** | **Skills Objectives** |
| --- | --- | --- |
| **Unit 1 Test** | • Determine the meanings of words.<br>• Understand that people belong to many different groups.<br>• Identify the responsibilities of authority figures in the school and home. | • Obtain information about a topic using pictures.<br>• Read and create a calendar.<br>• Understand that people belong to many different groups.<br>• Give examples of rules.<br>• Distinguish between past and present. |
| **Unit 2 Test** | • Determine the meanings of words.<br>• Give examples of how people in a neighborhood depend on each other.<br>• Understand similarities and differences between life in cities, towns, and on farms. | • Identify and describe the human characteristics of places such as types of houses.<br>• Construct a map using basic map symbols.<br>• Locate places using the four cardinal directions. |
| **Unit 3 Test** | • Determine the meanings of words.<br>• Describe the requirements of various jobs and the characteristics of a job well performed.<br>• Distinguish between needs and wants.<br>• Analyze picture and text to identify sequence.<br>• Obtain information about a topic using visual sources, such as graphics and pictures. | • Analyze pictures and text to identify sequence.<br>• Obtain information using visual sources.<br>• Use a simple map to identify the location of places.<br>• Locate places of significance on a map. |

|  | **Content Objectives** | **Skills Objectives** |
|---|---|---|
| **Unit 4 Test** | • Determine the meanings of words.<br>• Identify ways that natural resources can be used. | • Identify main ideas from print sources.<br>• Distinguish among past, present, and future.<br>• Create a time line.<br>• Identify physical features such as landforms and bodies of water.<br>• Distinguish between land and water on a map. |
| **Unit 5 Test** | • Determine the meanings of words.<br>• Identify contributions of historical figures who have influenced the nation.<br>• Obtain information about a topic from visual sources such as pictures. | • Use cardinal directions on a map.<br>• Obtain information about a topic from visual sources such as a diagram. |
| **Unit 6 Test** | • Determine the meanings of words.<br>• Obtain information about a topic from visual sources such as pictures.<br>• Identify the role of markets in the exchange of goods and services.<br>• Describe how household tools and appliances have changed.<br>• Describe how technology has changed communication.<br>• Identify the role of markets in the exchange of goods and services.<br>• Describe how household tools and appliances have changed.<br>• Describe how technology has changed transportation. | • Recognize words that help make a prediction.<br>• Create visual and written material, including graphs.<br>• Use a decision-making process to identify a situation that requires a decision. |

# NOTES

Name _____     Unit 1 Test

# Unit 1: Content Test

 Circle a word to finish each sentence.

1. The United States of America is a ____.
   country          school

2. I learn to read and write at ____.
   school           flag

3. My family is a ____.
   flag             group

4. My teacher makes ____ for the class.
   country          rules

5. There are stars and stripes on the ____.
   flag             rules

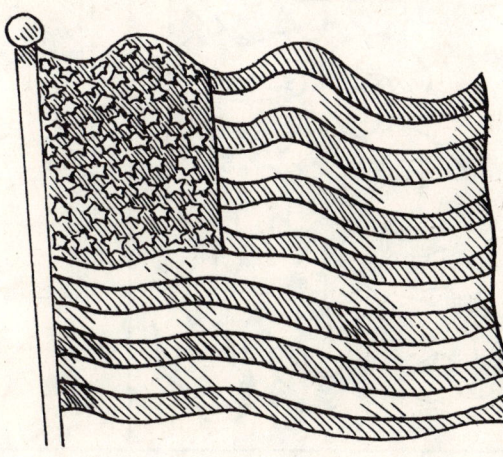

Name _____    Unit 1 Test

 **Draw** pictures of two groups you belong to.

 **Circle** people who help you follow school rules.

2  Unit 1 Test                              Assessment Book

Name _____

Unit 1 Test

# Unit 1: Skills Test

 **Circle** a clue that tells what time of day it is.

 **Write** an answer for each question.

## FEBRUARY

| Sunday | Monday | Tuesday | Wednesday | Thursday | Friday | Saturday |
|---|---|---|---|---|---|---|
| 1 | 2 | 3 | 4 | 5<br>Constitution Day–Mexico | 6 | 7<br>Dad's Birthday |
| 8<br>Susan's party | 9 | 10 | 11 | 12 | 13 | 14<br>Valentine's Day |
| 15 | 16 | 17 | 18 | 19 | 20 | 21 |
| 22 | 23<br>Presidents' Day | 24 | 25 | 26 | 27<br>Tony's class play | 28 |

What is the name of the month? _____

How many days are in this month? _____

On what day of the week is Presidents' Day? _____

Assessment Book         Unit 1 Test  **3**

Name _____

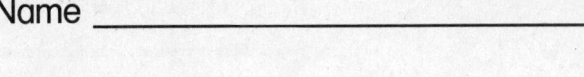

 **Circle** the picture that shows a group.

 **Draw** a line under a good rule for school.

Brush your teeth.

Raise your hand to talk.

Turn off the TV.

 **Circle** the picture that shows the past.

Name _____

Unit 2 Test

# Unit 2: Content Test

 **Circle** a word to finish each sentence.

1. North America is a ____.

   law                continent

2. Many neighborhoods make up my ____.

   community          ocean

3. A mayor is one kind of ____.

   state              leader

4. Atlantic is the name of a big ____.

   law                ocean

 Which word completes each sentence?

1. Littering is against the ____.

   a. leader          b. law

   c. ocean           d. state

2. Texas is a very big ____.

   a. leader          b. ocean

   c. continent       d. state

Name _____   Unit 2 Test

 Draw one person who helps in your neighborhood.
Draw a leader in your community.

|  |  |
|--|--|
|  |  |

 Circle a word to complete each sentence.

1. A town community is not as big as a ____.

   city               farm

2. Going to a parade on July 4th is a ____.

   law               custom

3. The United States is part of ____.

   Texas             North America

6  Unit 2 Test                                    Assessment Book

Name _____

Unit 2 Test

# Unit 2: Skills Test

 Color the two houses that are alike.

 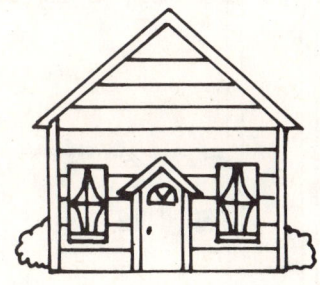 

Color the school red.

Color the park green.

Color the lake blue.

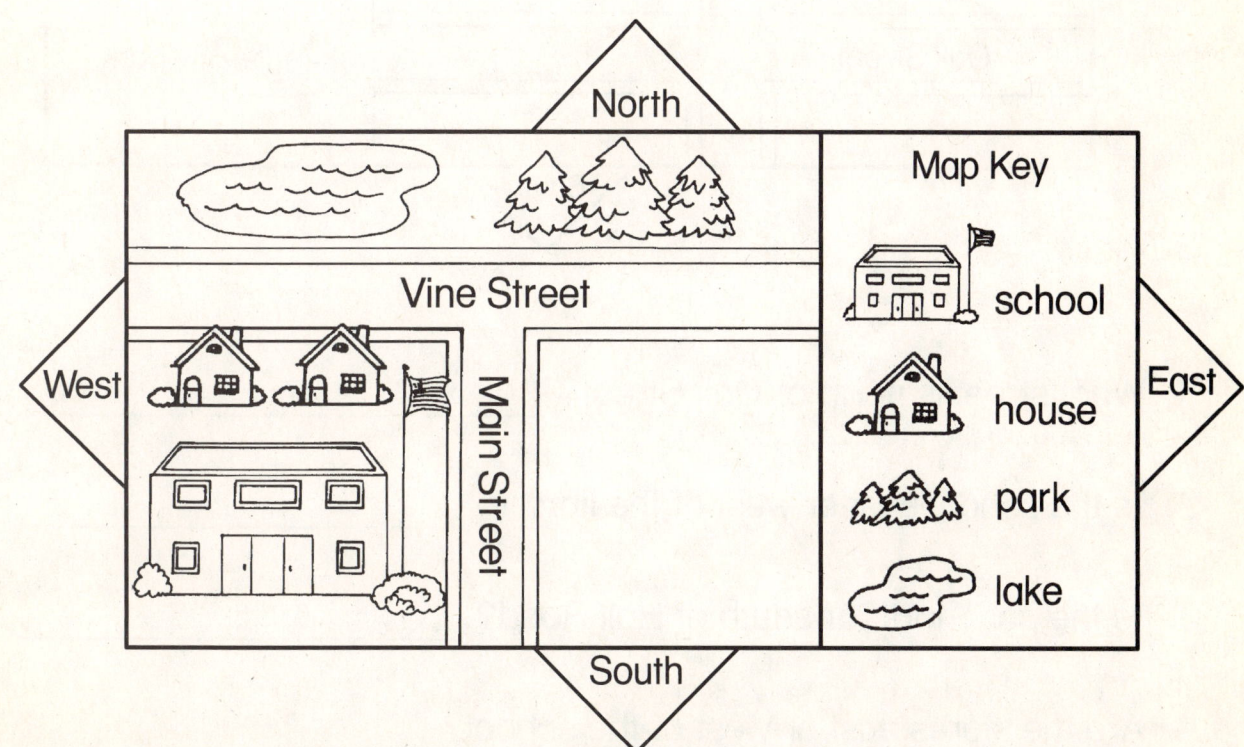

Assessment Book

Unit 2 Test  **7**

Name _____   Unit 2 Test

 **Look** at the map.

 **Write** an answer for each question.

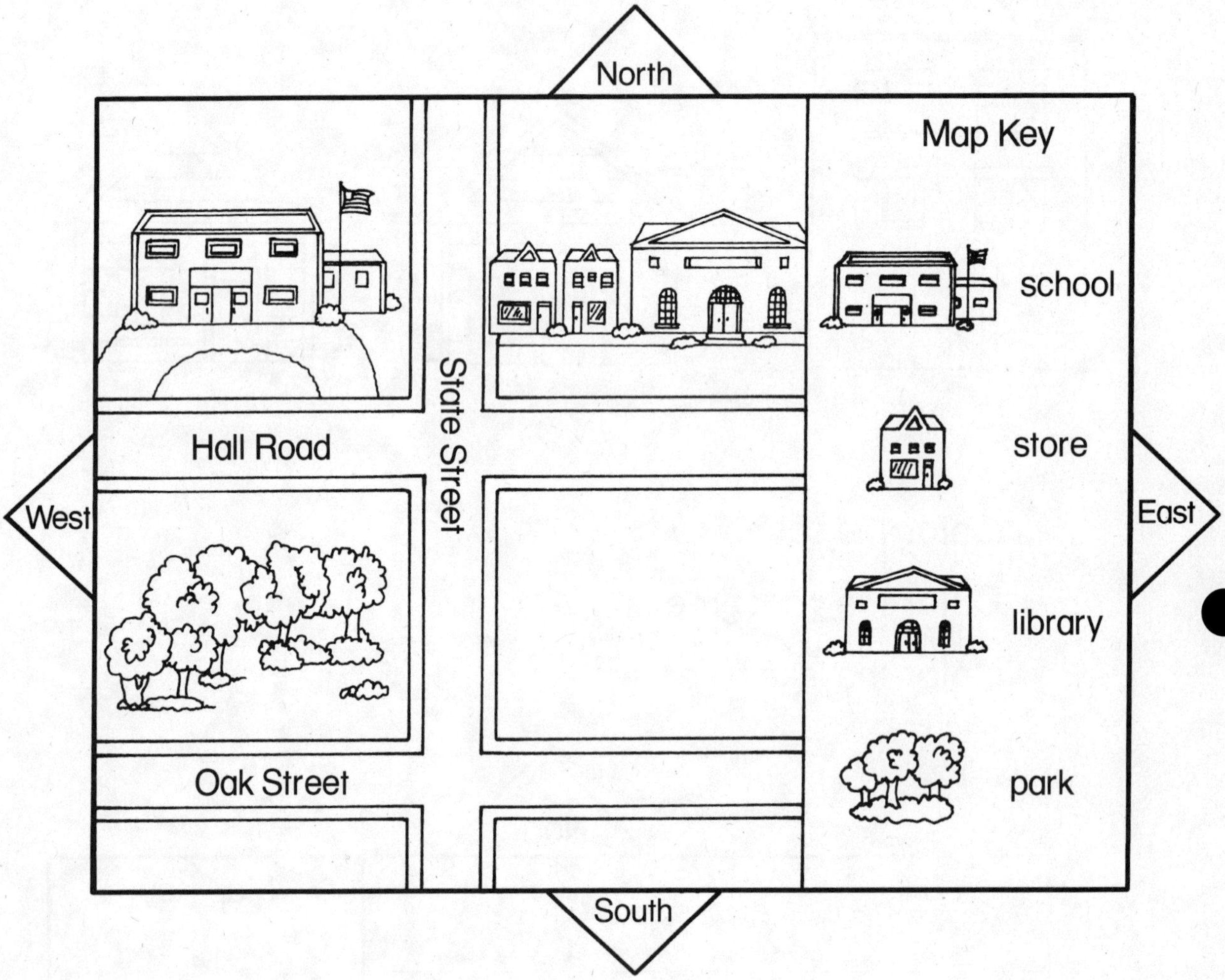

1. What street is north of Oak Street? _____

2. Is the school east or west of the library? _____

3. Is the park north or south of Hall Road? _____

4. Are the stores east or west of the school? _____

Name _____

Unit 3 Test

# Unit 3: Content Test

 **Circle** a word to finish each sentence.

1. Food, water, and clothing are ____.

   needs      jobs      volunteers

2. Toys, games, and TV are ____.

   needs      tools      wants

3. Hammers and nails are a builder's ____.

   tools      service      transportation

4. Cars, trucks, and vans are kinds of ____.

   needs      jobs      transportation

 Which word completes each sentence?

1. A person who works for free is a ____.

   a. job      b. volunteer

   c. service      d. transportation

2. Things that are grown or made are ____.

   a. goods      b. wants

   c. needs      d. tools

Name _____     Unit 3 Test

 **Draw** someone making or growing goods.
**Draw** someone doing a service job.

| Goods | Services |
|---|---|
|  |  |

**Draw** a line under the answer to each question.

1. Which is a need?                        toys         food

2. What is your job at school?             to learn     to eat

3. What can you do with money?             cook it      save it

4. Who grows the food we eat?              farmers      teachers

5. Which is a kind of transportation?      a house      a truck

Name _____

Unit 3 Test

# Unit 3: Skills Test

 **Write** *first*, *next*, and *last* to show the order.

_____     _____     _____

 **Write** names of people at home.

## Jobs at Home

| Jobs | Helpers |
|---|---|
| Set the table. | |
| Make the beds. | |
| Cook dinner. | |

Name _____

Unit 3 Test

Trace Lee's route on the map.

 **Write** words to complete the sentences.

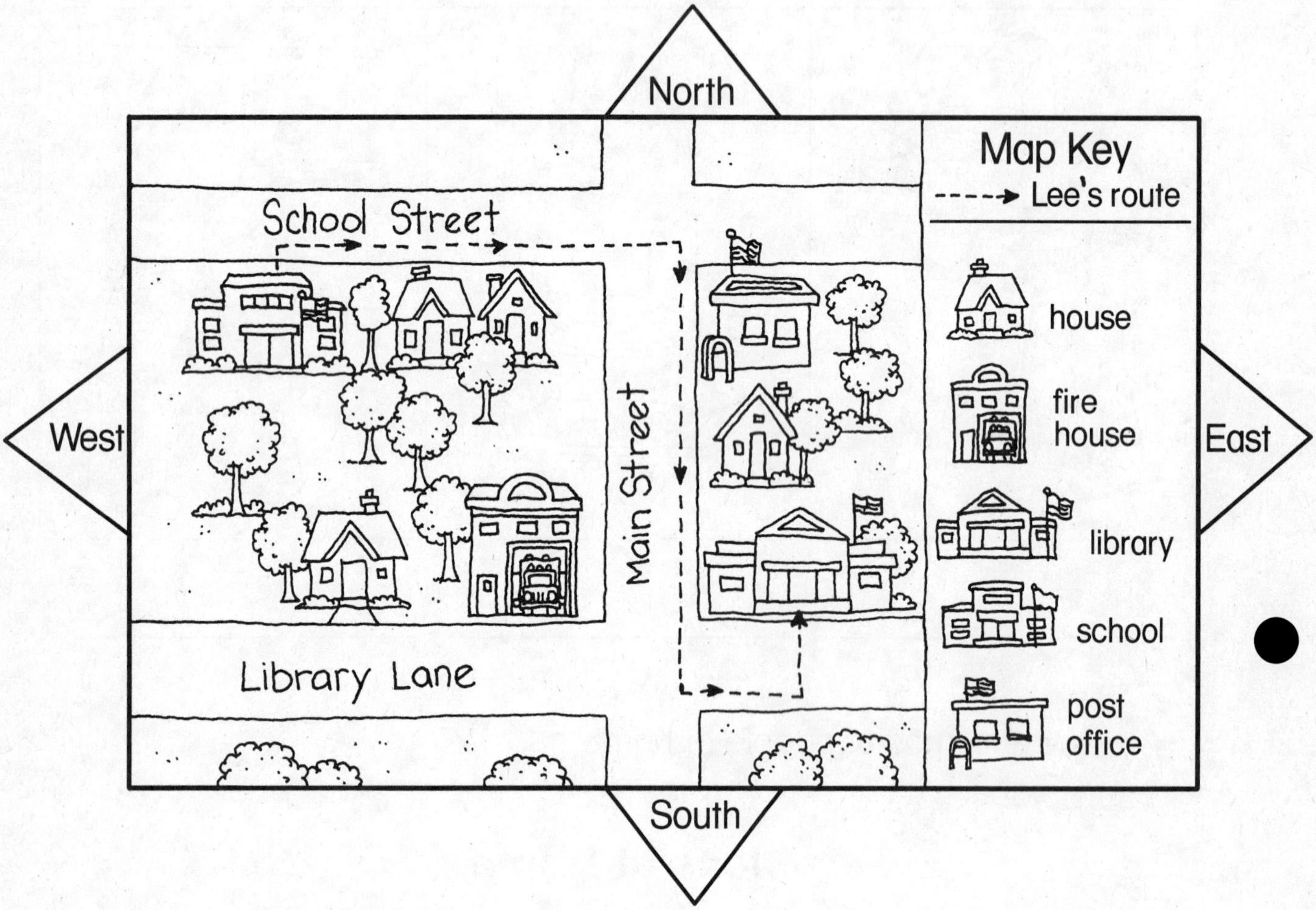

[Map showing North, South, East, West with School Street, Main Street, Library Lane, and a Map Key indicating Lee's route, house, fire house, library, school, post office]

1. Lee starts at the _____.

2. Lee goes _____ on School Street.

3. Lee goes _____ on Main Street.

4. Lee goes _____ on Library Lane.

**12**  Unit 3 Test                    Assessment Book

Name _____

Unit 4 Test

# Unit 4: Content Test

 **Circle** a word to finish each sentence.

1. A hill is not so high as a ____.

   lake          mountain

2. An ocean is much bigger than a ____.

   natural resource     lake

3. Air, water, and soil are examples of ____.

   endangered     natural resources

4. The water in a ____ usually moves toward a lake or the ocean.

   lake          river

 Which word completes the sentence?

1. For days now, the ____ has been rainy.

   a. weather          b. natural resource
   c. history          d. river

2. That book tells the ____ of our state.

   a. mountain         b. history
   c. plain            d. lake

Name _____

Unit 4 Test

 **Write** how you use each natural resource.

air _____

water _____

soil _____

gas _____

 **Draw** how you can help save a natural resource.

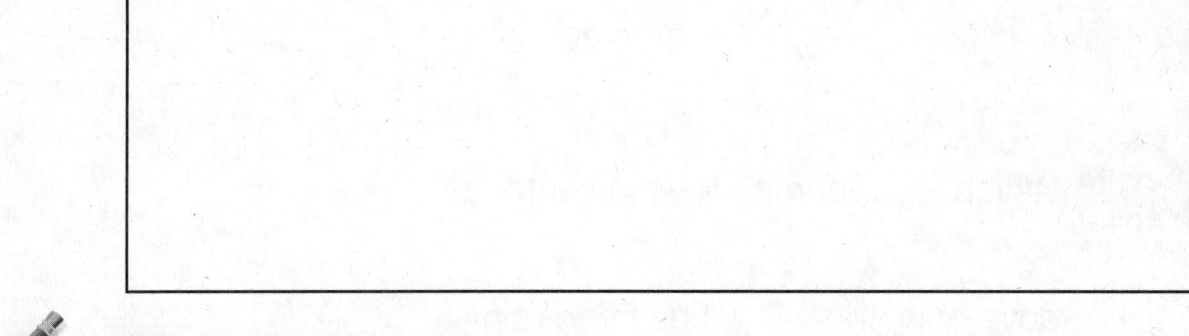

 **Draw** a line under the answer to each question.

1. Which is a large body of salt water?   pond   ocean   hill

2. Which do we get from trees?   oil   corn   paper

3. Who were the first farmers in Iowa?   Seneca   Ioway   Shoshone

4. What can you recycle at school?   cans   water   paint

Name _____   Unit 4 Test

# Unit 4: Skills Test

 **Look** at the picture and read the story.

    Jim wants to save trees. He doesn't take paper he doesn't need. When he writes, he writes on both sides. He uses the recycling bin to throw paper away. That way, the paper can be made into something for Jim to use again.

 **Draw** a line under the main idea of the story.

    Jim hikes in the woods.

    Jim wants to save trees.

    Jim is a good writer.

 **Draw** to show what you did each day.

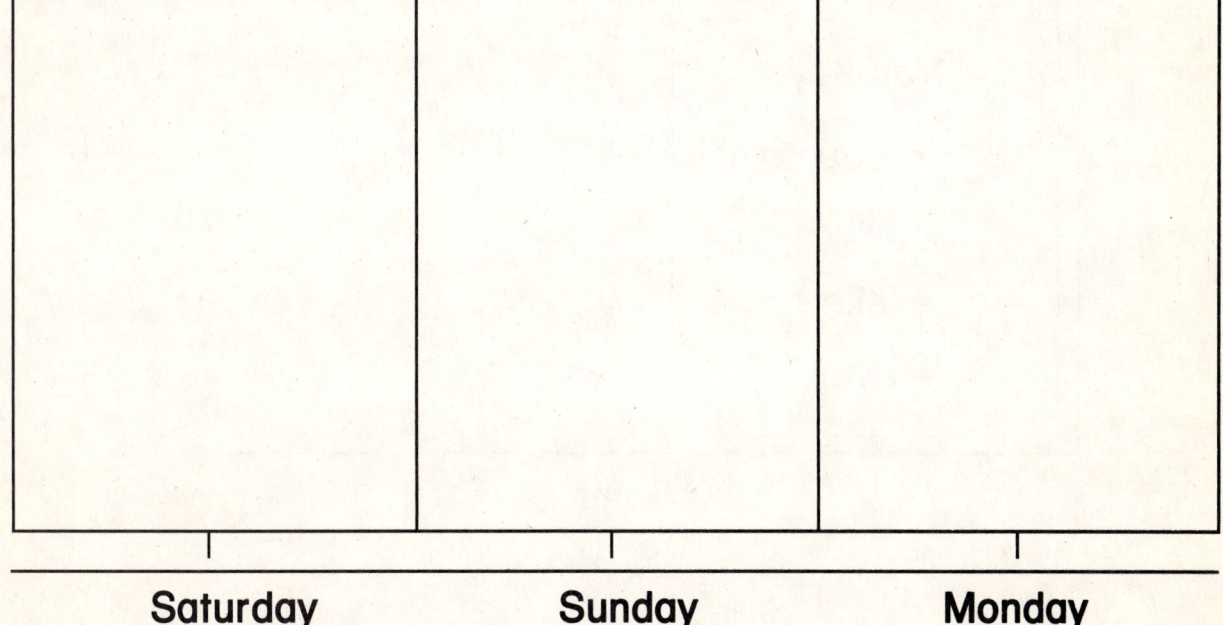

    Saturday          Sunday          Monday

Name _____

Unit 4 Test

 **Draw** symbols on the map key.
Then use the key to make a map.

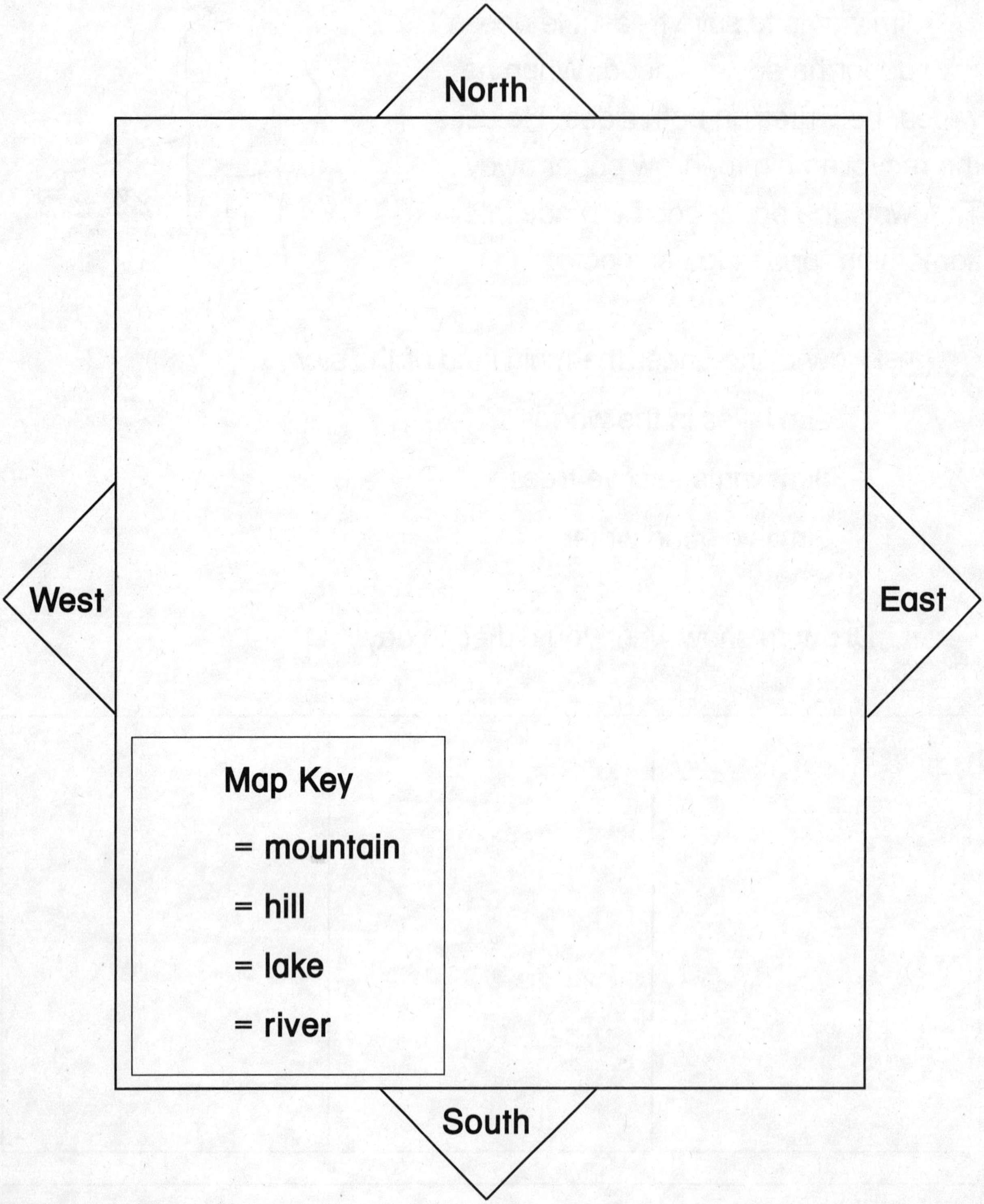

North

West

East

Map Key

  = mountain
  = hill
  = lake
  = river

South

**16** Unit 4 Test

Assessment Book

Name _____

Unit 5 Test

# Unit 5: Contest Test

 **Circle** a word to finish each sentence.

1. Indianapolis is the ____ of the state of Indiana.

   capital          colony          vote

2. To vote, a ____ of the United States must be 18 years old.

   holiday          colony          citizen

3. Presidents' Day is a ____ in February.

   freedom          holiday          colony

4. A person's right to make choices is called ____.

   freedom          capital          holiday

 Which word completes the sentence?

1. Virginia was once a ____ of England.

   a. vote          b. colony

   c. holiday       d. capital

2. George Washington was our first ____.

   a. citizen       b. capital

   c. holiday       d. President

Assessment Book

Unit 5 Test **17**

Name _____

**Unit 5 Test**

 **Write** a letter to match each picture with a sentence.

a. The first people in North America were Native Americans.

b. Columbus landed on an island near North America in 1492.

c. The Pilgrims came to North America on the *Mayflower*.

d. Women who lived in the colonies made their own candles.

e. George Washington was a famous leader during a war with England.

f. We have holidays to honor people from the past.

 **Write** to complete this sentence.

I am a citizen of the state of _____

and the country of _____ .

Name _____

Unit 5 Test

# Unit 5: Skills Test

 **Draw** three pictures to retell this story.

That first winter was very hard for the Pilgrims. The Wampanoag helped the Pilgrims. They showed Pilgrims what crops to plant. The Pilgrims hunted and fished for other food. Later, they celebrated with the Wampanoag.

| 1 | 2 | 3 |
|---|---|---|
|   |   |   |

 **Circle** the correct words.

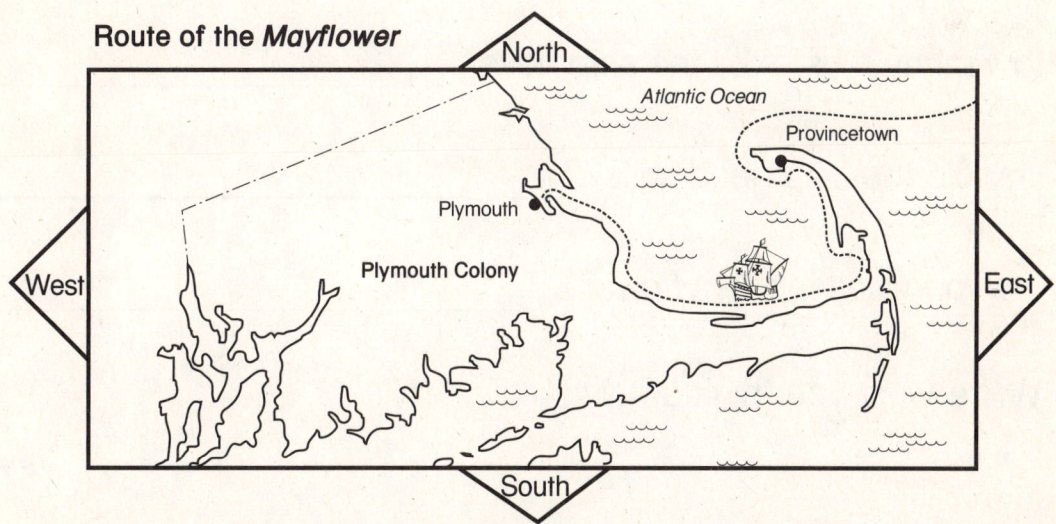

The Pilgrims sailed across the (Atlantic, Pacific) Ocean.

They landed first at (Boston, Provincetown).

They finally settled at (Plymouth, Boston).

Name _____  Unit 5 Test

**Answer** the questions about the diagram.

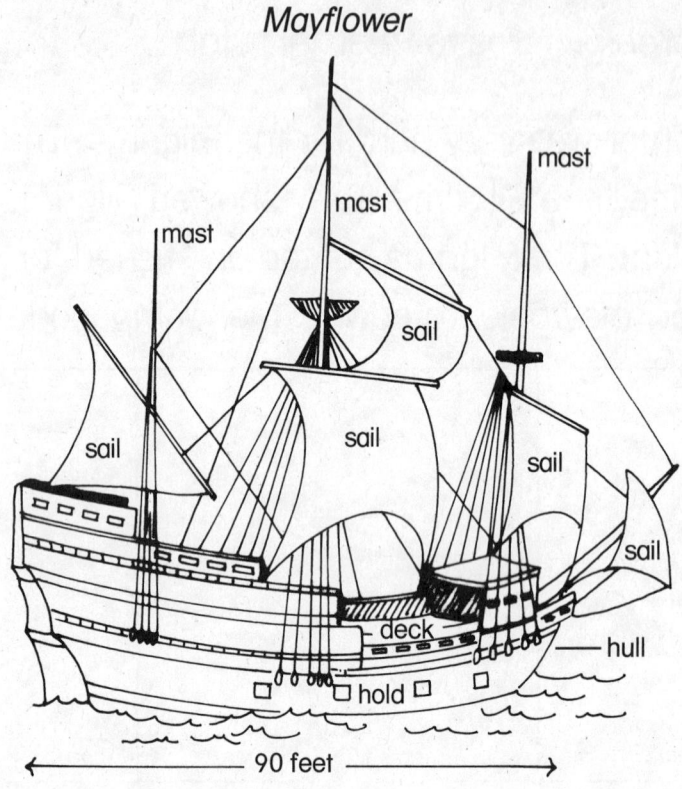

1. What does the diagram show? _____

2. How many masts did the ship have? _____

3. Why did the ship need sails? _____

4. How long was the *Mayflower*? _____

**Write** what you think of this ship.

_____

_____

_____

Name _____

Unit 6 Test

# Unit 6: Content Test

 **Write** a word from the box to finish each sentence.

> market   communicate
> world    invention

1. Earth is the name of our _____.

2. The printing press was a great _____.

3. Talking is one way to _____.

4. Goods are bought and sold at a _____.

 Which word completes the sentence?

1. People who invent things are ____.

   a. worlds      b. markets

   c. inventors   d. inventions

2. People use telephones to ____.

   a. invention      b. world

   c. communicate    d. inventor

Assessment Book           Unit 6 Test   **21**

Name _____

Unit 6 Test

 **Look** at each picture, and read the question.

 **Circle** the letter of your answer.

1. What do people do here?
   a. buy things they need
   b. make decorations
   c. borrow books to read

2. What looks very old?
   a. the sink
   b. the TV set
   c. the stove

3. Who invented this?
   a. Thomas Edison
   b. Alexander Bell
   c. Mae Jemison

 **Write** to complete these sentences.

Long ago, people traveled by _____.

Today, people travel by _____.

22 Unit 6 Test　　　　Assessment Book

Name _____

**Unit 6 Test**

# Unit 6: Skills Test

 Write to predict.

Luis has a pen pal. The pen pal lives in Japan. Luis and his pen pal write to each other often. They tell each other about their families and friends.

One day, Luis got a new pet. He was so excited! He drew a picture of his dog. He put himself in the picture too.

What will Luis do?

_____

Use the bar graph to answer the questions.

## Best Pets

| | | | | | |
|---|---|---|---|---|---|
| Dogs | | | | | |
| Cats | | | | | |
| Fish | | | | | |
| Birds | | | | | |
| | 1 | 2 | 3 | 4 | 5 |

How many children like dogs? _____

How many children like fish? _____

What pet do the children like best? _____

Assessment Book          Unit 6 Test  **23**

Name _____

**Unit 6 Test**

 **Write** to answer the question.

Nan needs to make a decision. Her family wants a pet. Dad wants a cat. Mom wants a dog. Nan isn't sure what she wants.

What decision does Nan's family need to make?

_____

 **Circle** 4 other steps Nan's family should take.

Let one person decide.

Gather information.

Wait for a week to decide.

List the choices.

Tell what might happen with each choice.

Make a decision.

Name _____  Unit 1 Test

## Unit 1: Content Test

✏️ Circle a word to finish each sentence.

1. The United States of America is a ____.
   (country)    school

2. I learn to read and write at ____.
   (school)    flag

3. My family is a ____.
   flag    (group)

4. My teacher makes ____ for the class.
   country    (rules)

5. There are stars and stripes on the ____.
   (flag)    rules

Assessment Book                Unit 1 Test  **1**

---

Name _____  Unit 1 Test

✏️ Draw pictures of two groups you belong to.

| Drawings will vary. | |
|---|---|
|   |   |

✏️ Circle people who help you follow school rules.

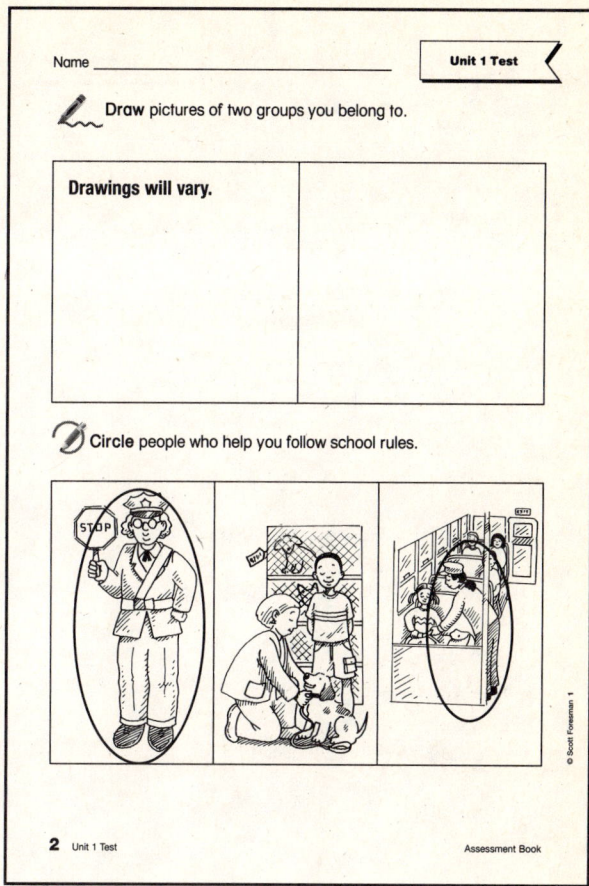

**2**  Unit 1 Test                Assessment Book

---

Name _____  Unit 1 Test

## Unit 1: Skills Test

✏️ Circle a clue that tells what time of day it is.

✏️ Write an answer for each question.

What is the name of the month?  __February__
How many days are in this month?  __28__
On what day of the week is Presidents' Day?  __Monday__

Assessment Book                Unit 1 Test  **3**

---

Name _____  Unit 1 Test

✏️ Circle the picture that shows a group.

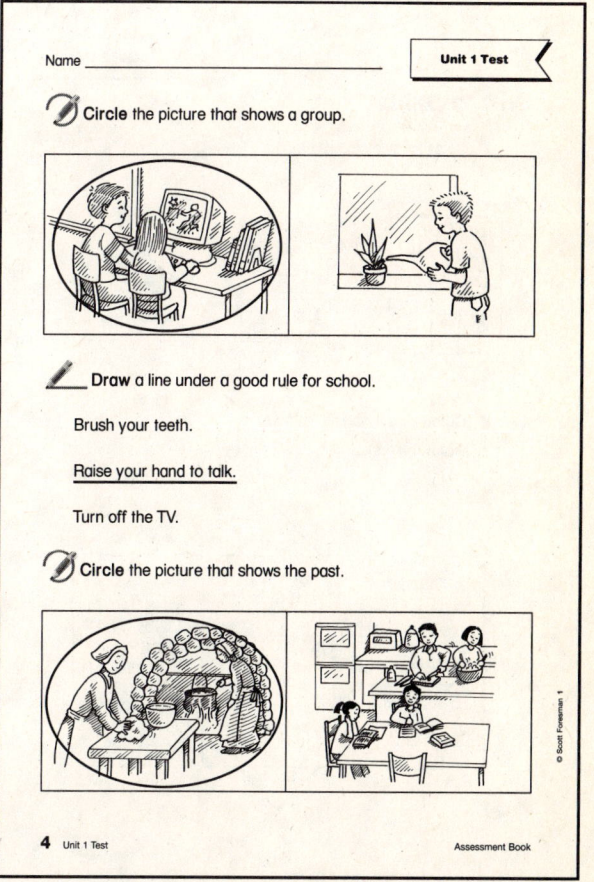

✏️ Draw a line under a good rule for school.

Brush your teeth.

__Raise your hand to talk.__

Turn off the TV.

✏️ Circle the picture that shows the past.

**4**  Unit 1 Test                Assessment Book

---

Assessment Book                Answer Key  **25**

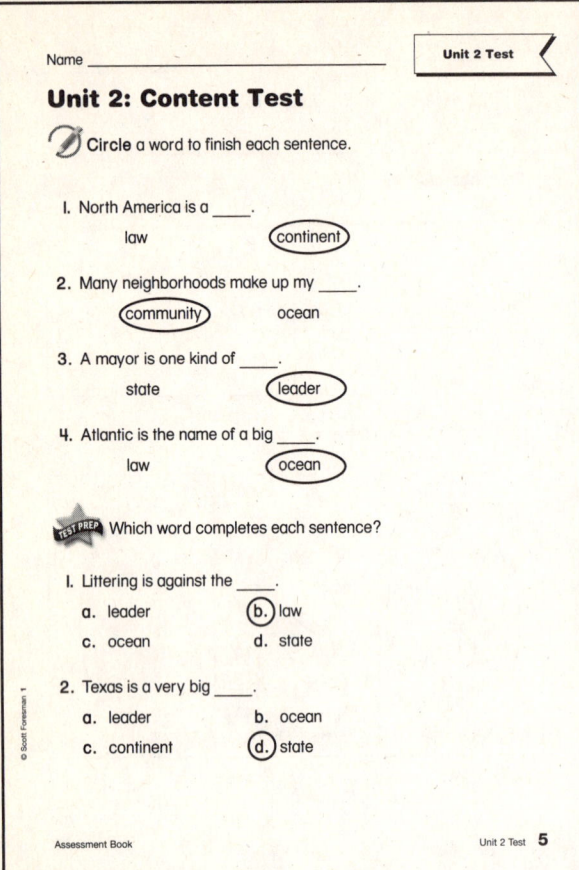

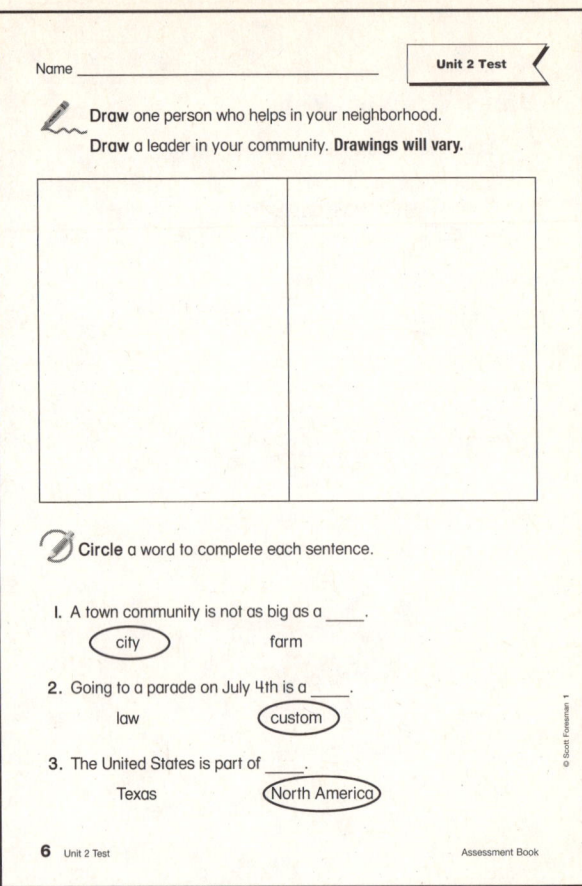

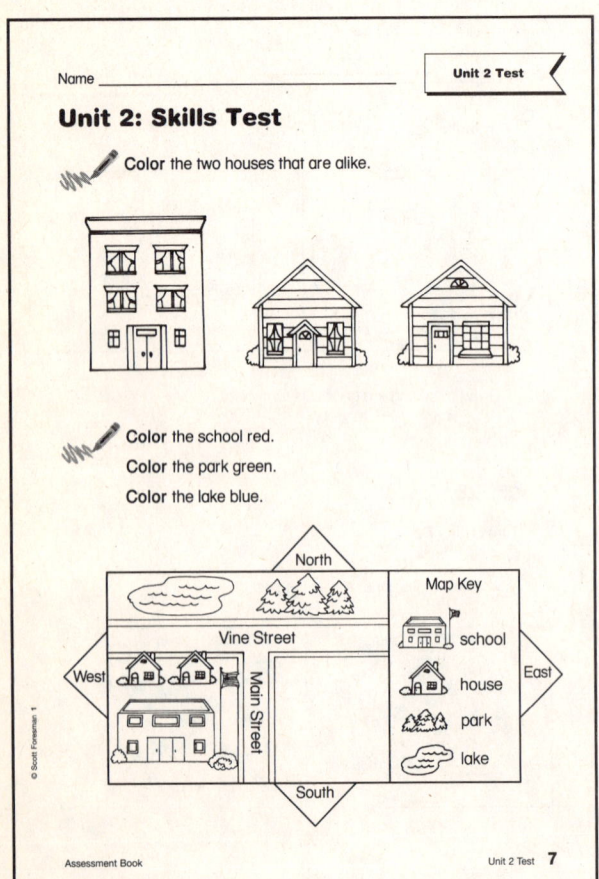

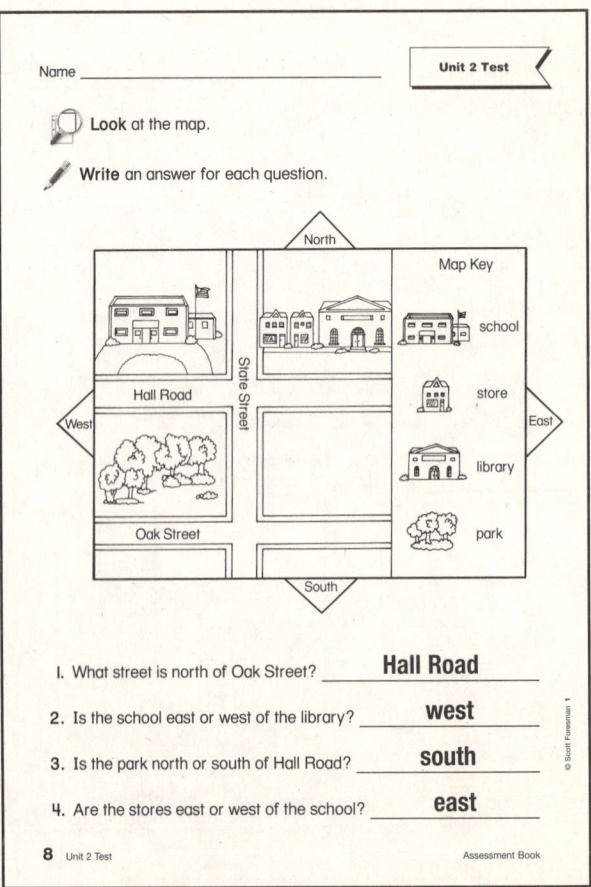

**26** Answer Key

Name _____     Unit 3 Test

## Unit 3: Content Test

*Circle* a word to finish each sentence.

1. Food, water, and clothing are ____.
   (needs)      jobs      volunteers

2. Toys, games, and TV are ____.
   needs      tools      (wants)

3. Hammers and nails are a builder's ____.
   (tools)      service      transportation

4. Cars, trucks, and vans are kinds of ____.
   needs      jobs      (transportation)

**TEST PREP** Which word completes each sentence?

1. A person who works for free is a ____.
   a. job      (b.) volunteer
   c. service      d. transportation

2. Things that are grown or made are ____.
   (a.) goods      b. wants
   c. needs      d. tools

Assessment Book          Unit 3 Test  9

---

Name _____     Unit 3 Test

*Draw* someone making or growing goods.
*Draw* someone doing a service job. **Drawings will vary.**

| Goods | Services |
|-------|----------|
|       |          |

*Draw* a line under the answer to each question.

1. Which is a need?                      toys        <u>food</u>
2. What is your job at school?           <u>to learn</u>   to eat
3. What can you do with money?           cook it     <u>save it</u>
4. Who grows the food we eat?            <u>farmers</u>   teachers
5. Which is a kind of transportation?    a house     <u>a truck</u>

10  Unit 3 Test          Assessment Book

---

Name _____     Unit 3 Test

## Unit 3: Skills Test

*Write* first, next, and last to show the order.

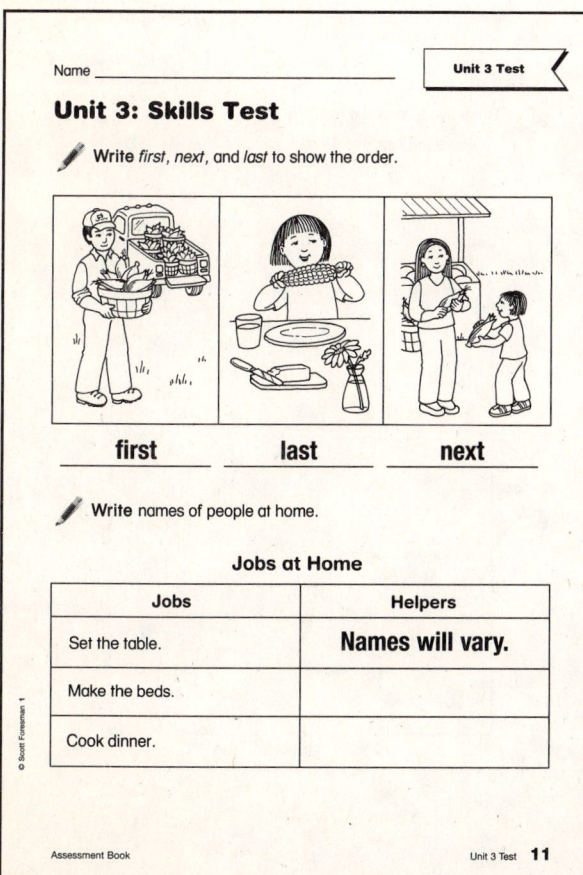

first          last          next

*Write* names of people at home.

### Jobs at Home

| Jobs | Helpers |
|------|---------|
| Set the table. | **Names will vary.** |
| Make the beds. |  |
| Cook dinner. |  |

Assessment Book          Unit 3 Test  11

---

Name _____     Unit 3 Test

Trace Lee's route on the map.
*Write* words to complete the sentences.

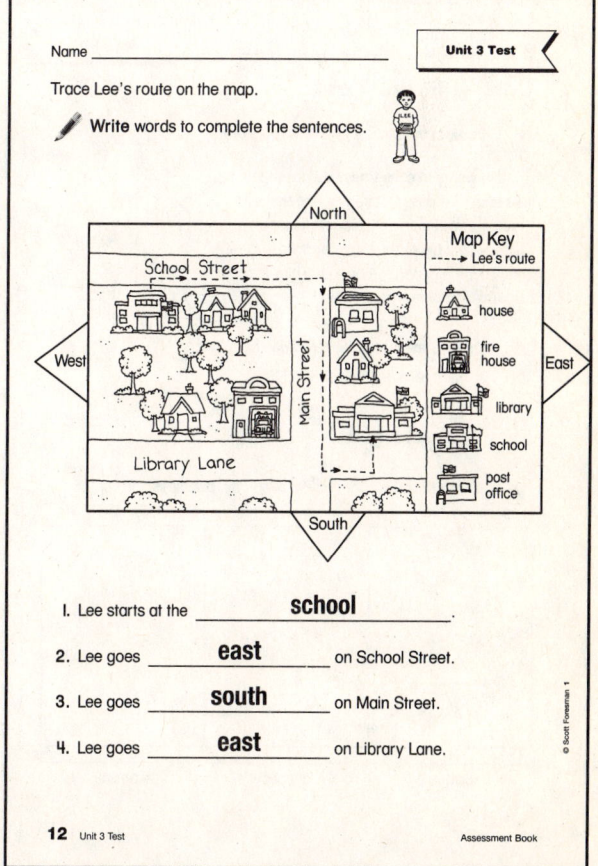

1. Lee starts at the ____school____.
2. Lee goes ____east____ on School Street.
3. Lee goes ____south____ on Main Street.
4. Lee goes ____east____ on Library Lane.

Answer Key **27**

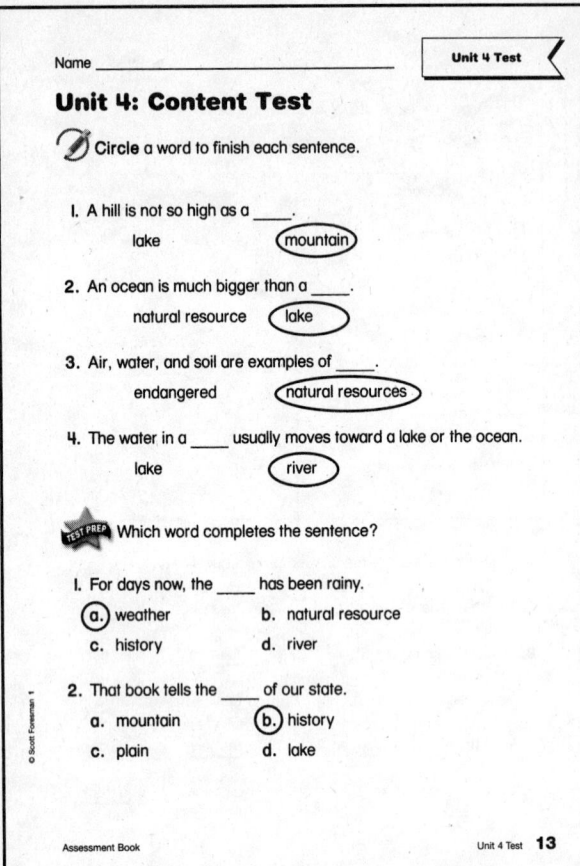

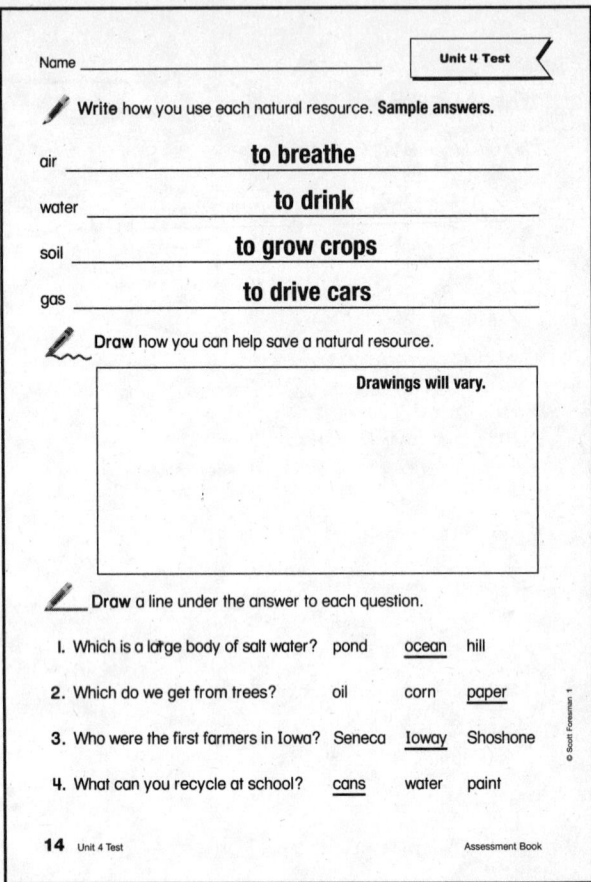

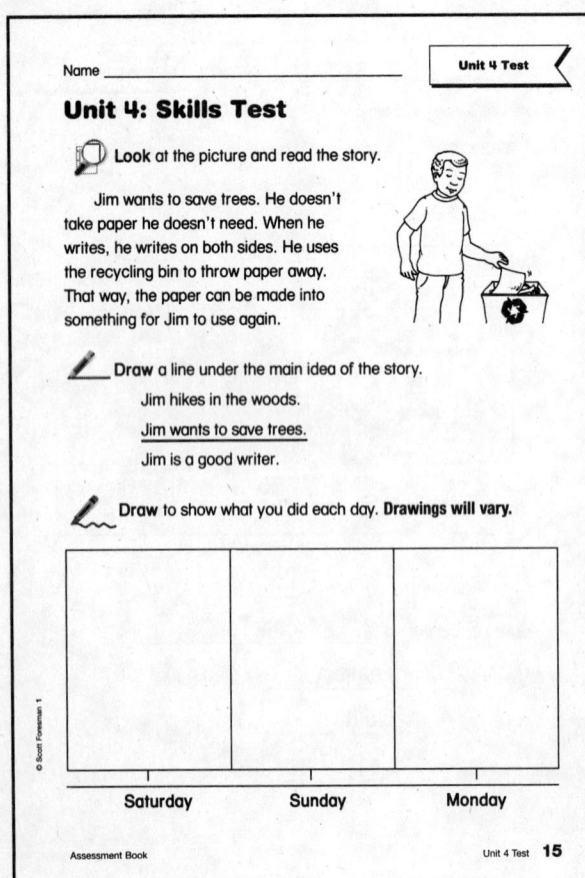

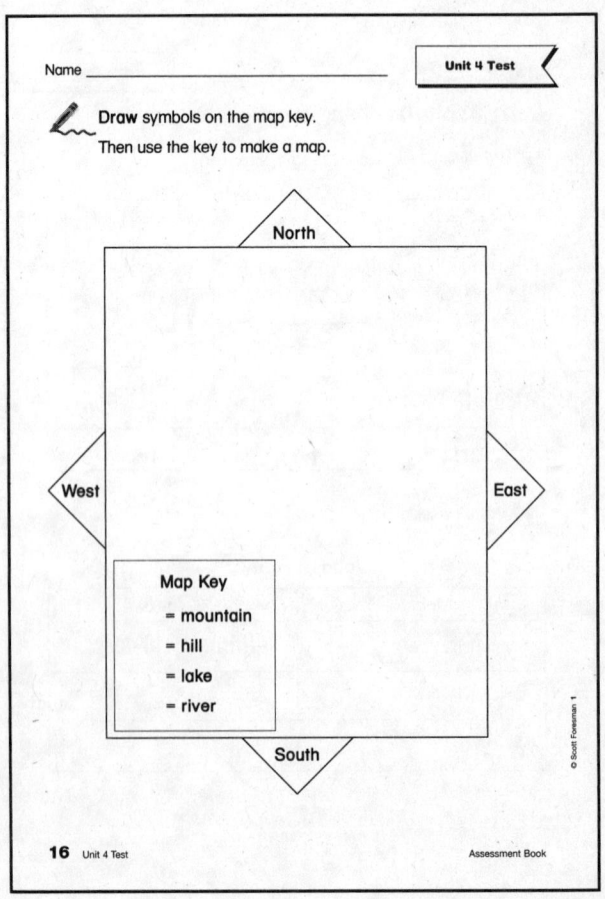

28  Answer Key                                   Assessment Book

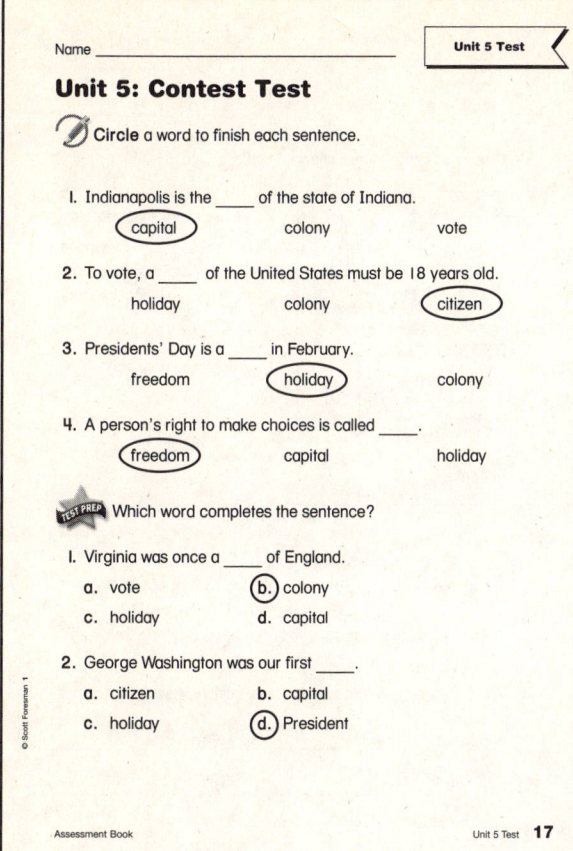
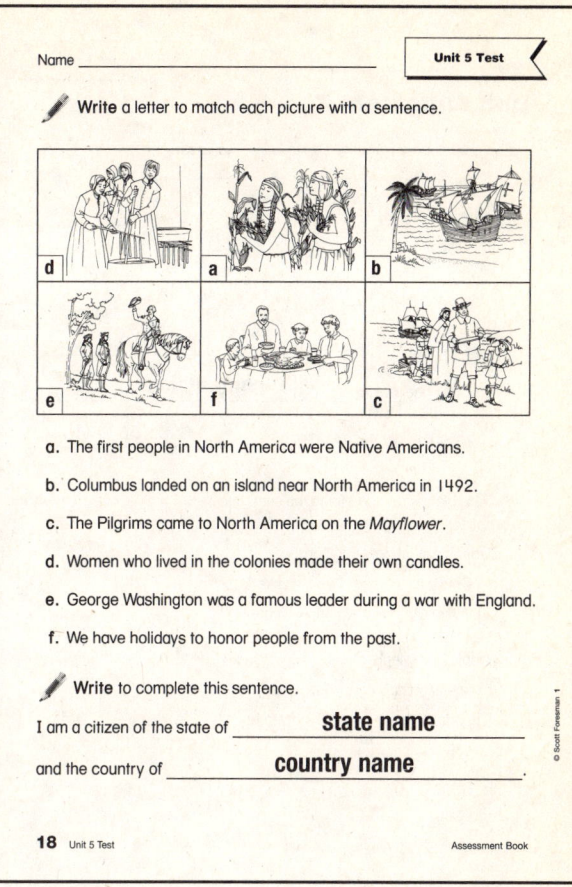
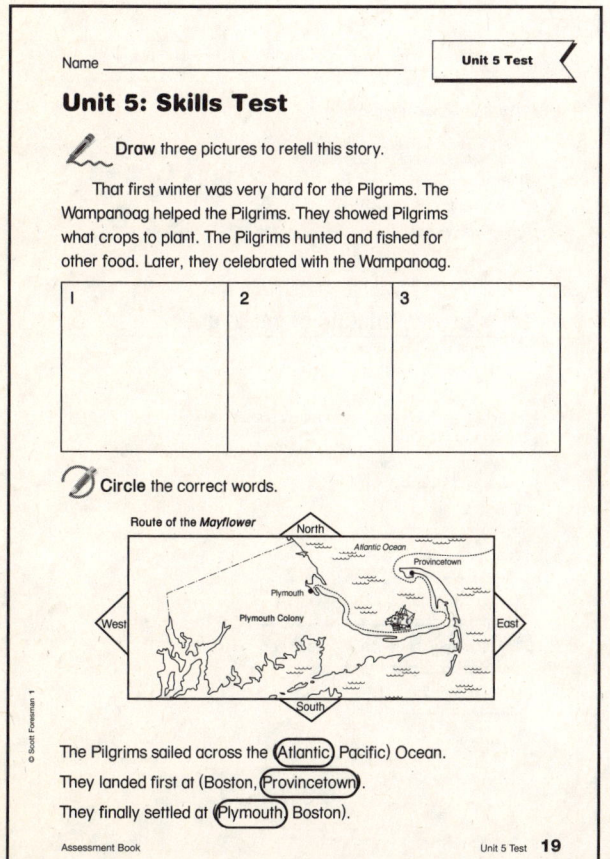
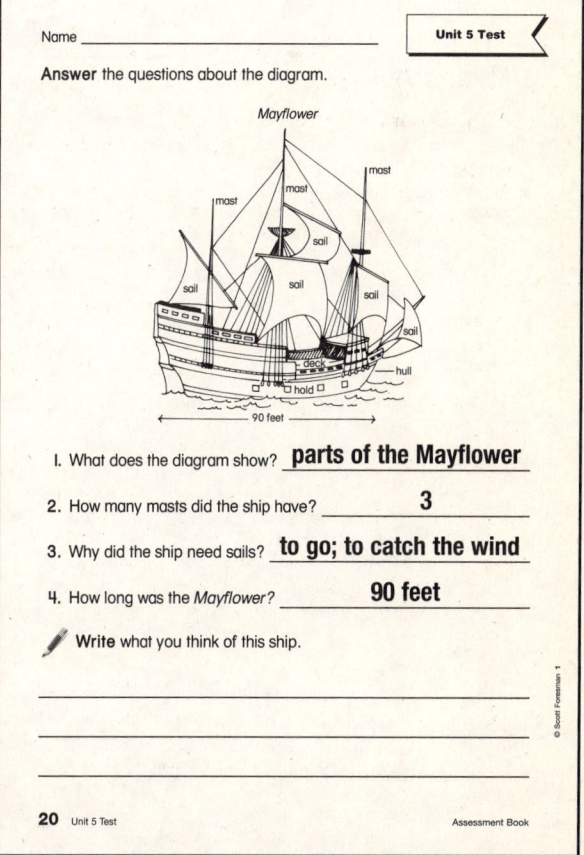

Name _____  Unit 6 Test

## Unit 6: Content Test

Write a word from the box to finish each sentence.

| market | communicate |
| world | invention |

1. Earth is the name of our ___**world**___
2. The printing press was a great ___**invention**___
3. Talking is one way to ___**communicate**___
4. Goods are bought and sold at a ___**market**___

**TEST PREP** Which word completes the sentence?

1. People who invent things are ____.
   a. worlds  b. markets
   (c.) inventors  d. inventions

2. People use telephones to ____.
   a. invention  b. world
   (c.) communicate  d. inventor

---

Name _____  Unit 6 Test

Look at each picture, and read the question.
Circle the letter of your answer.

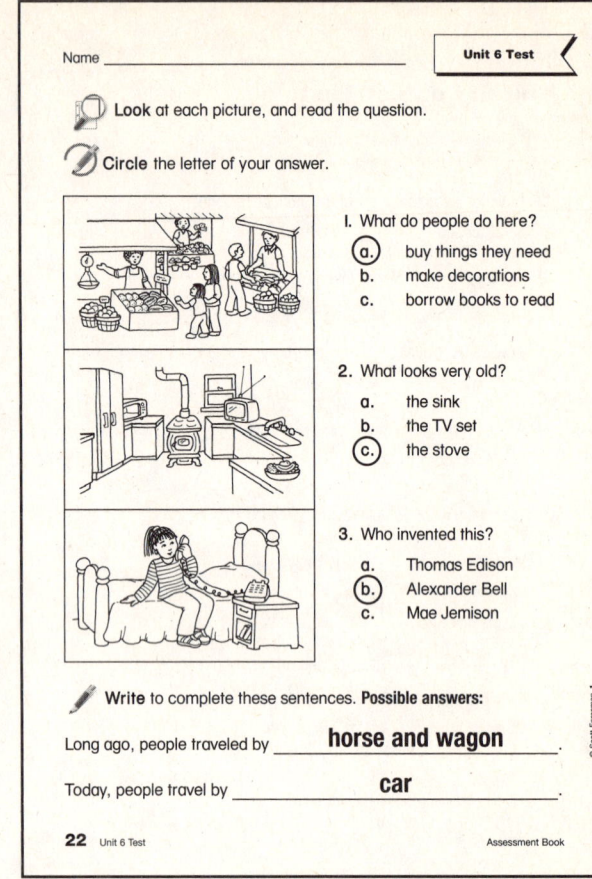

1. What do people do here?
   (a.) buy things they need
   b. make decorations
   c. borrow books to read

2. What looks very old?
   a. the sink
   b. the TV set
   (c.) the stove

3. Who invented this?
   a. Thomas Edison
   (b.) Alexander Bell
   c. Mae Jemison

Write to complete these sentences. **Possible answers:**

Long ago, people traveled by ___**horse and wagon**___.

Today, people travel by ___**car**___.

---

Name _____  Unit 6 Test

## Unit 6: Skills Test

Write to predict.

Luis has a pen pal. The pen pal lives in Japan. Luis and his pen pal write to each other often. They tell each other about their families and friends.

One day, Luis got a new pet. He was so excited! He drew a picture of his dog. He put himself in the picture too.

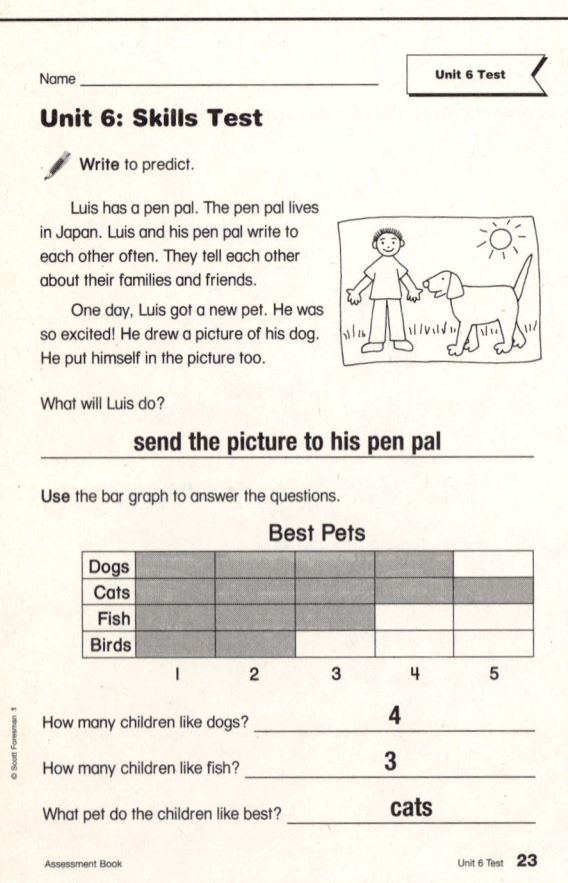

What will Luis do?

___**send the picture to his pen pal**___

Use the bar graph to answer the questions.

**Best Pets**

| Dogs | | | | | |
| Cats | | | | | |
| Fish | | | | | |
| Birds | | | | | |
| | 1 | 2 | 3 | 4 | 5 |

How many children like dogs? ___**4**___
How many children like fish? ___**3**___
What pet do the children like best? ___**cats**___

---

Name _____  Unit 6 Test

Write to answer the question.

Nan needs to make a decision. Her family wants a pet. Dad wants a cat. Mom wants a dog. Nan isn't sure what she wants.

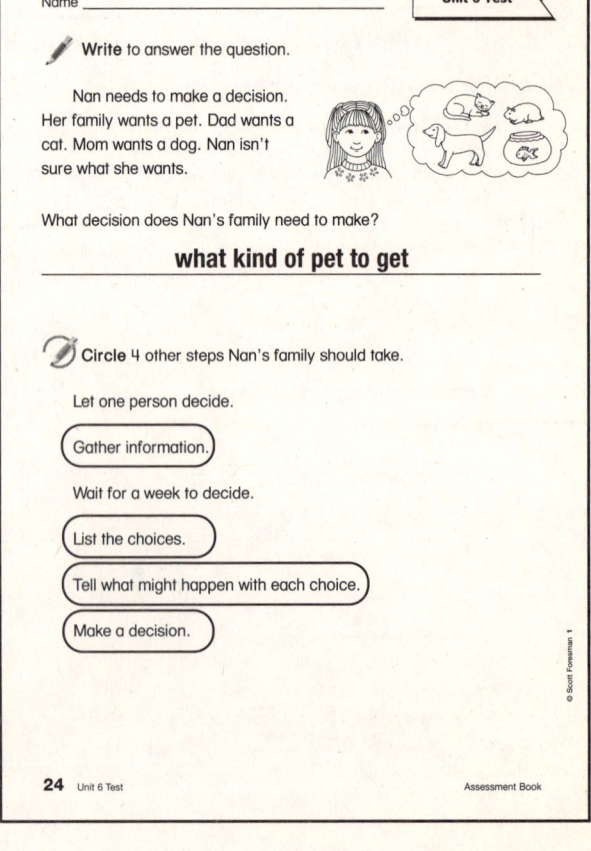

What decision does Nan's family need to make?

___**what kind of pet to get**___

Circle 4 other steps Nan's family should take.

Let one person decide.

(Gather information.)

Wait for a week to decide.

(List the choices.)

(Tell what might happen with each choice.)

(Make a decision.)

---

**30** Answer Key

# NOTES

# NOTES

# NOTES

# NOTES

# NOTES

# NOTES

# NOTES

# NOTES

# NOTES

# NOTES